The Anti Hustle

BE STILL DARLING

a four week devotional
encouraging
the pursuit of God + rest

Sethlina
AMAKYE

Introduction

He says, Be still, and know that I am God
Psalms 46:10 (NIV)

Since early 2015, I have meditated upon this verse almost to the point of an obsession. In the beginning, be still, which eventually turned into *Be Still Darling*, was a cute saying I put on my handmade pillows and candles found in my store. It was an homage to a favorite childhood verse, one of the first I had ever memorized.

I knew somewhere in 2016 that this scripture was supposed to be taken personally, but it felt impossible and contradictory to my real life. *He couldn't possibly understand.* Stillness felt like a distant request that was far-fetched and unattainable.

Why would God be stalking me with this verse?
I get it.
I'm doing too much.
I'll slow down, Jesus. Eventually.

Y'all, I tried to move on to another piece of scripture. I promise I did. I soon learned that God, in His mercy, would use this same annoyance of a verse to save my life just two years later.

In 2017, I had a booming custom home goods business while operating a well-received women's ministry. I was asked to speak all over the Dallas-Fort Worth metroplex in addition to several out of state engagements. It was not unusual for me to work with celebrity clientele. I couldn't believe it. I was finally able to witness what two years of hard work and sleepless nights could produce.

In the meantime, I couldn't fully appreciate the newfound success. Behind the scenes, I was falling apart. I experienced daily anxiety attacks, flu like symptoms for extended periods of time, fainting spells, a 30-pound weight gain that nobody could diagnose, debilitating depression, boils in my armpits for months at a time, and my blood pressure numbers had doctors surprised I hadn't fallen over dead yet. I was a complete and total mess.

The world teaches that hustling and grinding is the only way to make it. I have a feeling your heart knows better. I don't believe it's by mistake that you picked up this devotional.

There is something about going against the grain, The Anti-Hustle, that your soul longs for. The very idea that it is possible to have peace and serenity that passes all understanding while living out your biggest dreams feels like a cold drink in a desert, doesn't it?

This devotional is a culmination of everything I've learned over the past few years, and the answers God gave me in my darkest moments. It has saved my life, and I am convinced that it will be transformational for you as well. As we go through the next four weeks together, I pray that you can see that God didn't design you to hustle, at least not the modern definition of it. He has so much more in store for you!

Before we begin week #1, allow me to clarify a few things. I originally wrote this as a four chapter, 4-week mini devotional and still feel it is most effective when read a chapter a week. Since then, I've had a change of heart about restricting it to a weekly process. An essential part of The Anti-Hustle is understanding when to push and when to slow down and reflect. Although it is still separated into weeks, I am going to rely on the Holy Spirit to lead you. If you feel led to read it in one sitting, please do, but also be open to needing two weeks to digest one chapter.

I don't know if you are a mother reading this while breastfeeding or a student using this as a quick devotional before you get to Calculus. Whatever phase of life you are in, all I ask is that you say an earnest pray before diving in. Ask God to show you where to slow down. Ask the Holy Spirit for an extra dosage of discernment to not reject a

truth that may need re-reading. Ask Him to show you where modifying your lifestyle can be more beneficial in aligning with His word.

I've been there. I've rushed through something to get it over with, missing crucial parts intended just for me. I'm going to trust that you will get precisely what you need, no matter how you choose to process it.

Devotional Features

Here are a few additions to help you navigate through the book. Following your weekly devotional, you will find three sections:

1. **My Note to Self:** I often use a Note-to-Self format as part of a personal journaling method. Sometimes I write it to my future self and sometimes it is addressed to my past self. These notes combine to create The Anti-Hustle Manifesto that I pray blesses you as much as it has blessed me over the years.

2. **Application**: Use these questions to gain clarity and apply newfound truths to your life. I know, you're going to feel tempted to skip over it. Do it anyways. (If you are reading this as a digital copy, consider journaling the answers)

3. **Your Note to Self**: Here is a chance for you to write a Note to Self of your own! Choose your past,

present, or future self and pen a note from your heart. (Again, feel free to journal this if reading this from a screen)

That it! Let's get started.

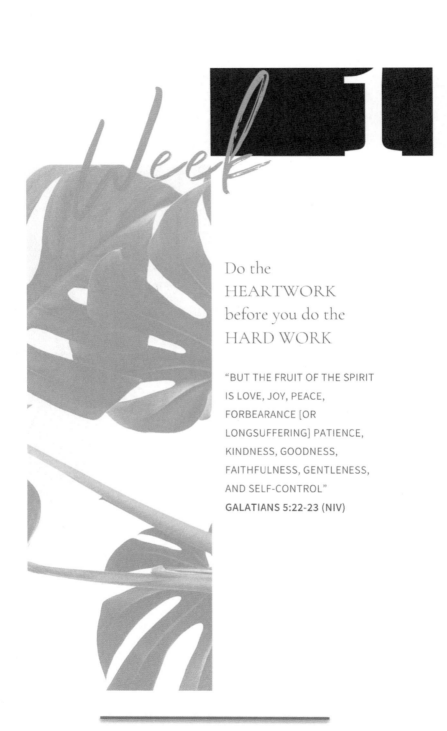

Week 1

Do the
HEARTWORK
before you do the
HARD WORK

"BUT THE FRUIT OF THE SPIRIT
IS LOVE, JOY, PEACE,
FORBEARANCE [OR
LONGSUFFERING] PATIENCE,
KINDNESS, GOODNESS,
FAITHFULNESS, GENTLENESS,
AND SELF-CONTROL"
GALATIANS 5:22-23 (NIV)

For a long time, I walked around with a skewed view of what God wanted for me. The running narrative was that He cared more about what I did and less about who I was. I had to unlearn the lie to understand His plan for my life.

> For the Lord sees not as man sees: man looks on the outward appearance, but the Lord looks on the heart.
> 1 Samuel 16:7 (ESV)

He doesn't care about my version of His plan for me.
He cares about the intention.
He cares about my character.
He cares about my "why" (As in, what is motivation or my reason to do what I am dreaming of doing?)
He cares my about obedience.

truth bomb

Your WHY has nothing to do with wealth. It may be a "by-product," but it doesn't have to be connected to money for God to use it for His glory. Purpose is not a contractual agreement for monetization.

God is amazing and intentional. He is the creator and giver of dreams (*See Joseph: Genesis 37-50*). He purposely gives us a vision that is beyond the reach and capability of our small human hands. The enormity of it requires us to give it back to Him knowing we can't do it alone. God-sized dreams push us to believe for greater!

In the meantime, we wonder if we are even allowed to dream that big. We think about it all day and can't wait for Him to open the "promised" door...or window.

That dream is different depending on who you are. It could be a dream for a successful business or future relationship. It could be wealth, notoriety, or influence. It could be homeownership or something as simple, but no less important, as growing out your edges or nails. As you can see, there is nothing wrong with dreaming and praying that God orders our steps to achieve them. The problem happens when we get off track and obsess about the incorrect details. The details that so easily derail us.

This might be a good time to tell you a bit about my story. For as long as I can remember, I have felt "called" to something greater. I understand that because of who our Father is, we are *all* called to more, but my calling felt personal and distinct. I had a deep longing to do great things, but my circumstances said otherwise. In 2007, several events coincided at the same time.

- *My father was diagnosed with leukemia.* He won the first time, went into remission, and it came back with a vengeance. We lost him soon after.

- *I was on my 3rd crazy abusive relationship* because, for whatever reason, I kept falling in love with the typical played out "bad boy" trope. It was tiring, and yet, there I was, a glutton for punishment.

- *I dropped out of college without telling anyone.* I still showed up on campus every day because I didn't want people to be disappointed by my lack of focus and indecision. I honestly didn't know what career path I wanted to choose and felt immense pressure to be something worthy of the expectation placed upon me.

In short, I was falling apart. During this time, I had an experience with God that changed my life. Pictures this:

I'm beyond drunk at a club in downtown Cleveland. I had just thrown up my expensive pasta dinner in the sketchiest women's restroom, and somehow made it across the dance floor to the unused VIP lounge area. There I was in and out of sleep on a sticky leather couch in the back of the room panicking as my mind started to entertain dark thoughts like, *what if I die back here?*

Right there at that moment, I mumbled something that resembled a prayer, wondering if the loudspeakers were blocking my desperate request to heaven. I remember feeling sad and worried, wondering if God could hear me over the DJ playing Chris Brown and T-Pain.

I said something along the lines of, *Jesus, there's must be more to life than this. Tell me what it is. I don't want to be like this anymore.* Within seconds, I felt someone put a hand on my shoulder, so I looked up assuming it was security. No one was there. I laid back down and closed my eyes and had a vision that outlined the rest of my life. I couldn't believe it. Jesus showed up and sat right down next to me on that ugly faux leather couch and handed me the blueprint.

I spent the next ten years fixated on what I had seen that night. Every detour towards that dream became a crippling defeat instead of a lesson learned. I would fall apart at the smallest sign of failure and found myself making decisions that did not align with the original plan just to expedite the outcome. *I must be disappointing Him. He gave this to the wrong person.*

Even small wins became a catastrophic weight. I was deathly afraid of messing up again and often self-sabotaged success without thinking about it. After I got tired of running into the same outcome, I began to ask the hard questions. *Why was I so impatient? Who was I trying to prove something to? Why did I feel unworthy?* After much prayer, I discovered that I had been doing it wrong all along.

I discovered a part of me was still that scared inebriated girl on the couch. My worth was still tied to sketchy life choices and a bottle of tequila that I hadn't touched in years.

May I submit to you that in the pursuit of our God-sized dreams, we rarely leave room for the pruning of character? Let me explain.

My mother is an avid gardener. Over the years, it has taught me about what it takes to have a bountiful harvest. I've seen her take a plant that I would assume was dead and instead, take out a pair of gardening shears and lovingly cut off several branches. She calls it pruning. Just days later, you can see buds where it looked like nothing could become of it. When I would have easily and quickly rushed to declare it dead, she sees an opportunity to make room for growth. This concept reminds me of John 16: 1-2 (NIV) where Jesus says:

> I am the true vine, and my Father is the gardener.
> He cuts off every branch in me that bears no fruit,
> while every branch that does bear fruit, he prunes so
> that it will be even more fruitful.

While God was cutting dead branches from me, I went straight into working on what I believed He had promised me, and I could have cared less about what He was trying to do within. God knew I had not yet dealt with the trauma I had experienced the years prior. I had a lot of baggage that needed some major unpacking. It meant that any success I gained could not stand long term. I was feeling burnout because my priorities were not in alignment. I wanted the gift more than the Giver. I wanted my dream more than the original Dreamer.

Character is foundational for the blessings He has in store for you. It is how we can be trusted to handle things with excellence and integrity. It is how we ensure that we come out at the other end, purified and ready to walk in the fullness of His favor. However, because character formation (holiness) is hard work, it's easier to focus on the dream: how it's going to manifest, the specific amount of favor and blessings needed to operate smoothly, the people involved, and the monetary value attached.

> Therefore, since we have these promises, dear friends,
> let us purify ourselves from everything that
> contaminates body and spirit, perfecting holiness
> out of reverence for God.
> 2 Corinthians 7:1 (NIV)

Here is how we like to think about the manifestation of what we are called to:

Our Point of View:

God told me that one day I'm going to be in a position of influence. He's going to expand my territory by making me go viral. I'll meet Oprah, and she'll tell everyone about me. That's how the whole world will know I am blessed.

God's Point of View:

That's not what I said. I'm going to teach you submission and patience at your 9-5 (under the boss you hate) FIRST. The way you treat him or her (despite the way they treat you) will plant a seed that will be watered in the future. Your elevation will come because of Jesus, IN you. Your SPIRITUAL growth will be the key that opens the door that no man can shut.

Do you see how that is nothing like what we want to imagine for ourselves? That second scenario takes patience...you know, like the Fruit of the Spirit kind of patience [long-suffering or forbearance]. It takes time, and as a culture, we have learned to despise anything that takes time.

Friend, I curated a timeline and running order based on ovaries, cash flow, and love interests without God's full blessing. I idolized the dream and put it on a pedestal for all to see:

I'm not that girl anymore!
Look at how He's blessing me!

The sad thing is, I still felt empty. I was hustling to be seen and affirmed, all the while becoming increasingly unhappy with the results. I was desperately trying to separate myself from who I used to be instead of taking God's hand and walking into my healing step by step; I didn't want to bother Him. I thought I could do it on my own. Sound familiar?

It's time to rearrange our pursuit of the world/vision we have assigned to ourselves and replace it with a heart after His. Above all things, He wants our heart.

> My [son/daughter], give me your heart and
> let your eyes delight in my ways.
> Proverbs 23:26 (NIV)

How beautiful is that? Once we give our hearts to Jesus, our eyes begin to delight in HIS ways. The vision He gave us begins to mirror what HE sees for us, and how it will impact Kingdom work. When we start to see it for ourselves, we ultimately feel full by merely doing it His way and in the correct order.

David learned this lesson well. He knew that God had promoted him to the highest position in the land, but his heart had not been prepared for the elevation. I believe this is why he so easily lusted after another man's wife (2 Samuel 11).

Can you believe a man chosen to be King from a young age still felt the need to take matters into his own hands? As if God hadn't shown him that it was handled and that He didn't need David's help? He messed up royally, pun intended. Somewhere inside; he was still the overlooked shepherd boy in the pasture waiting to be seen (1 Samuel 16).

There were still bits of trauma that needed pruning. Hindsight, of course, is always 20/20. We may not realize how pieces of our past affect the future, that is until we are looking at ourselves in the mirror wondering why we reacted the way we did. Later, when the psalmist writes in Psalms 51, I feel his anguish:

Purify me from my sins, and I will be clean; wash me, and I will be whiter than snow. Oh, give me back my joy again; you have broken me— now let me rejoice. Create in me a clean heart, O God. Renew a steadfast spirit within me

It's all about our character and HEART, one of complete reliance and brokenness before God, even when traumatic experiences in your past rear their ugly head.

I am not a betting type of woman, but if I were, I would be willing to bet everything on this fact: Your "hustle" is going to be way different when you look at it from the perspective of a broken spirit placed in the hands of the Potter. Your drive and reasoning won't look or feel the same. Your motives will come to the surface, and there will be some ugly gunk that you didn't realize was in there, but it will all be worth it. You will be ready for whatever God has planned for you.

Do the HEART WORK before you do the HARD WORK. Be equally intentional, if not more intentional, about pursuing a life that is after God's heart as you are about the hustle.

Sidebar: Don't be afraid of therapy. You can love Jesus and still need a clinician to help you work your way through it all.

As you read through these pages, I would love for you to focus less on the hustle of attaining the dream and more on being prepared for it by acknowledging your past hurts and developing the Fruit of the Spirit:
love, joy, peace, patience, kindness, goodness, faithfulness, gentleness, and self-control.

Our Father is waiting to give us a clean heart so that as things begin to fall into place, we are more concerned about how to ensure our character is planted with deep roots in Christ.

One of my favorite hymns my daddy used to sing all the time is based on Psalms 139:23. The lyrics are written by J Edwin Orr and says:

Search me, O God, and know my heart today,
Try me, O Savior, know my thoughts, I pray;
See if there be some wicked way in me;
Cleanse me from every sin and set me free.
(Search Me, O God, 1936)

The heart-work is actually "harder" than building an empire. The heart-work is eternal. Can you imagine God granting you the desires of your heart as you are simultaneously becoming a better sister, daughter, wife, friend, co-worker, etc.?

Ask Him to search your heart and prune anything that is in the way. When things finally begin to fall into place and your purpose becomes clear, you will be more concerned about how to ensure your character is planted with deep roots *in* Christ long term.

Application

Write down your biggest dream(s). *The one that makes your heart beat a little faster when you think about it.*

_____

Application

What parts of your character may need some additional development? *Use the Fruit of the Spirit as a guide*

Application

In what ways do your dream(s) point people to Christ?
How can your dream(s) be transformative to your own
character and pursuit of heaven?

Note to Self

Galatians 5:22-23 (NIV)

But the fruit of the Spirit is love, joy, peace, forbearance [or long suffering) patience, kindness, goodness, faithfulness, gentleness, and self-control.

1 Samuel 16:7 (ESV)

For the Lord sees not as man sees: man looks on the outward appearance, but the Lord looks on the heart.

John 16: 1-2 (NIV)

I am the true vine, and my Father is the gardener. He cuts off every branch in me that bears no fruit, while every branch that does bear fruit, he prunes so that it will be even more fruitful.

2 Corinthians 7:1 (NIV)

Therefore, since we have these promises, dear friends, let us purify ourselves from everything that contaminates body and spirit, perfecting holiness out of reverence for God.

Proverbs 23:26 (NIV)

My [son/daughter], give me your heart and let your eyes delight in my ways.

Psalm 51:7-12 & 17 (NLT)

Purify me from my sins, and I will be clean; wash me, and I will be whiter than snow. Oh, give me back my joy again; you have broken me— now let me rejoice. Create in me a lean heart, O God. Renew a steadfast spirit within me. Do not banish me from your presence, and don't take your Holy Spirit from me. Do not banish me from your presence, and don't take your Holy Spirit from me. Restore to me the joy of your salvation, and make me willing to obey you...

The sacrifice you desire is a broken spirit. You will not reject a broken and repentant heart, O God.

Week #1

NOTE TO SELF

I will not use the vision He gave me as a test of His goodness or faithfulness. He is GOD with or without my dream. He delights in giving me my heart's desire, but I will not forget whose desires they are to begin with. I will allow my character to be pruned and heart to be purified in preparation for what is to come. I will REST in the promise, knowing that it will come to pass, and He doesn't need my help to do so.

Week 2

Let God Be God
(Be Still, Darling)

AND IT CAME TO PASS, THAT ON THE MORROW MOSES WENT INTO THE TABERNACLE OF WITNESS; AND, BEHOLD, THE ROD OF AARON FOR THE HOUSE OF LEVI WAS BUDDED, AND BROUGHT FORTH BUDS, AND BLOOMED BLOSSOMS, AND YIELDED ALMONDS.

NUMBERS 17:8 (KJV)

Typically, when people are hustling, they are chasing a big, crazy, God-sized dream. Therefore, I tend to focus on the pursuit of goals and objectives when referring to rest, not because there aren't other areas in which we hustle, but hopes are a unifier. We all have them. They are what drives us to make specific decisions. We want to ensure that each step is in line with how we envision our lives for the foreseeable future.

Let me be fair. It's not the pursuit of the dream that I am asking us to re-examine. Our God made us in His image, and I would like to think that He is a dreamer himself, and dreams take work. What I am asking is for us to take a more in-depth look at the process of attaining that dream and what we are willing to do to secure it. There is a certain impatience that comes with the pursuit of goals (as we discussed last week).

Can I be honest here? I tend to be impatient about everything! I am good at rushing, grinding, moving, hustling, and absolutely the worst at waiting. Waiting puts me in the passenger seat with someone else controlling the steering wheel. It's way too risky and I always prefer to be in control of the narrative.

What if they turn the wrong way?
What if they drive too slowly?

The "Be Still, Darling" mantra is for me. It is as a reminder to myself to take several seats. It alludes to Psalm 46:10 (NIV) which says:

> Be still, and know that I am God;
> I will be exalted among the nations,
> I will be exalted in the earth.

As popular as the verse is, I found it difficult to apply practically. In certain seasons, it translated as the rest of the world rushing by as I missed my only chance. It was like being put on the bench in the middle of a championship game.

truth bomb

Impatience is a dream killer

How dare God make me sit when I could have made the winning shot?
Doesn't He want me to be happy?
Didn't He promise that I would be the head and not the tail?
I'm tired of not being seen. I'm tired of not being elevated.
I'm tired of watching everyone else make it.
I deserve to be on top.

Not only had the dream God gifted me for morphed into a selfish pursuit (based on what I thought I deserved), my misplaced motives and impatience exacerbated the long-term process of seeing "fruit" sprout from a seemingly impossible situation.

Here is this week's text one more time, and then additional context:

And it came to pass, that on the morrow Moses went into the tabernacle of witness; and, behold, the rod of Aaron for the house of Levi was budded, and brought forth buds, and bloomed, blossomed, and yielded almonds.
Numbers 17:8 (KJV)

Okay, here's the deal:

There were a few Levites who were upset about Moses and Aaron being chosen by God to lead. There were 3 gentlemen named Korah, Dathan, and Abiram, who started a rebellion in protest. God was not pleased. The rebels (with their families) were swallowed by the earth (Numbers 16:28-33).

You would think that would be the end, but wait, there's more. A few other knuckleheads kept the revolt going, and it started to spread amongst the people.

Aaron and Moses begged God not to swallow up the entire community, and God agreed.

Instead, He sent a plague that killed 14,700 Israelites. (Numbers 16:49)

To teach a lesson, God commanded Moses to have the leaders of each tribe bring their rod or staff to the Tent of Meeting (Aaron represented the tribe of Levi).
They each inscribed their names on their respective rods, and God told Moses.

> Buds will sprout on the staff belonging to the man I choose. Then I will finally put an end to the people's murmuring and complaining against you
> Numbers 17:5 (KJV)

Aaron's staff not only sprouted but also brought forth flowers *and* fruit (almonds).

A rod.
Placed inside a tent.
Budded, blossomed, bloomed, <u>AND</u> yielded almonds.

May I share a few facts you may not know about almonds? Almonds require a considerable amount of water. As a matter of fact, a single almond needs a little over 1.1 gallons of water to grow! Secondly, almond blossoms require cross-pollination. They are not self-fertile and require other tree varieties within their radius so that cross-fertilization can occur using bees. (I pray you are already connecting the dots!)

From a human point of view, the tent was an impossible situation. There was no source of water.

There were no other trees to cross-pollinate.

There was no soil and no outside source of natural light.

If you haven't caught on already, we serve a God of *intentional coincidences*. He specifically chose almonds due to the impossibility of growth where the rod was placed. There's no *way* the rod should have been able to produce fruit on its own.

I believe He wanted to ensure that the people understood and witnessed that it was GOD's doing and not man.

Contrary to popular belief, you don't need to work yourself into the ground to be seen or used by God. Your pursuit of whatever dream He gave you isn't just for you. It's for the rest of the world to see His glory THROUGH you. There is no "I" or "me" anywhere to be found in that thought process:

> Let your light shine before others, so that they may see your good works and give glory to your Father who is in heaven.
> Matthew 5:16 (KJV)

Our lights should shine so brightly that others see it and give Glory to God, but it must be HIS way. It must be according to HIS plan. Let me see if I can think of a relatable comparison.

I got it!
Let's bake a cake!

Pardon me, I've been binge-watching The Great British Baking Show on Netflix. For those of you unfamiliar with the show, it is only the best televised cooking competition of all time! At least, I think so.

The basic premise is amateur bakers from all over the United Kingdom meet for a series of high pressure and timed, baking challenges. It's so much fun to watch regular everyday people try their hands at some tough challenges. I typically get so caught up in the show that I am convinced, falsely of course, that I can make a three-tiered Strawberry and Rose Meringue from scratch in under 20 minutes. Hubris. The downfall of many a novice baker.

Now, back to my metaphor.

Alright, so you're ready to bake a cake of your own. You get the recipe, the supplies, mix all the ingredients, pour the batter into a well-greased cake pan, and place it into a preheated oven. You've done this before, executed it perfectly, and so you are confident that cake is about to be delicious.

You're licking the excess batter in the bowl in anticipation. You begin to smell something sweet in the atmosphere. So far, everything is going well!

Suddenly, you are aware that your next-door neighbor or sisters' best friend or a random person you follow on Instagram are also baking a cake. All of a sudden, baking for pleasure at your own pace turns into a competition, and you fall into a comparison trap.

You look around, and everyone else is icing their cake. Some are even eating it and sharing it amongst their friends. Oh, the accolades! Oh, the pride on their faces! *That should be me*, you murmur to yourself.

Crumbling under pressure, you decide to take the cake out of the oven earlier than instructed. The recipe clearly says bake for 35-45 minutes, but you figure, *Meh, it must have been a typo; The Baking Authority* (I'm not even sure if there is a baking authority but follow me here) *doesn't know what they are talking about.*

Ultimately, the cake comes out raw, and you're mad at God for allowing you to remove the cake without warning you first.

Do you get it? This a tasty metaphor for our dreams. God has given us the perfect recipe with all the ingredients perfectly portioned off, the exact temperature, and how long it should bake and cool. But we lack the courage to see it through. We want all He has for us, and we want it right now without wondering if our heart is prepared for such a responsibility.

Instead of rushing, let God do His job. In time, you will be shown the reason for the wait, and you'll wonder why you weren't patient all along.

We've got to stop chasing dreams without stopping to ask God for the blueprint. He chose *YOU* to see this thing through. He wanted *YOU* out of all the rods to blossom, bloom, and sprout almonds.

By the way, He's not asking you to dig a hole, find a source of water and figure out how to cross-pollinate yourself. He's asking you to have faith.

He wants to show you off!

He wants people to say, "Wow, that could only be God." I don't know about you but thinking about my dream this way was such a relief to my stressed-out heart.

Can we stop for a second and talk about the comparison trap? It's such a defining thing in this generation. It forces us to pursue lives that were not created for us. *It looks good on them so it will look even better on us!* That's a dangerous thought pattern that has destroyed many a good situation. It's called pride. We hate to say it that way, but it is what it is. We believe we know better than God, the creator of the universe.

Korah, Dathan, and Abiram weren't the first to assume they knew better. Lucifer was their predecessor. Often, we see Satan as a red, ugly being with a pitchfork and pointed ears. Sorry to mess up your idea for the next office costume party, but it's not true. The Biblical description of Lucifer will blow your mind:

You were in Eden, the garden of God; Every precious stone was your covering: The sardius, topaz, and diamond, Beryl, onyx, and jasper, Sapphire, turquoise, and emerald with gold. The workmanship of your timbrels and pipes Was prepared for you on the day you were created. You were the anointed cherub who covers; I established you; You were on the holy mountain of God; You walked back and forth in the midst of fiery stones. You were perfect in your ways from the day you were created, Till iniquity was found in you.
Ezekiel 28:13–15 (NKJV)

Y'all. Lucifer had diamonds as part of his skin! He was gorgeous! On top of that, he was "anointed" as one of the "cherubs who covers." This means that Lucifer, also known as "star of the morning," wasn't just a regular angel, he was kind of a big deal. My question is, how is it possible that he could fall into the comparison trap of wanting to be more. More than what? The most beautiful angel ever created?

We covered character last week, and I hope you see how lack of character development can allow negative traits to sneak into your heart? Pride can easily mess up a good thing.

> In his pride the wicked does not seek him;
> in all his thoughts there is no room for God.
> Psalm 10:4 (NIV)

Letting God be God takes a lot of humility. It is an act of submission that does not come easy to those of us that refuse to don't believe it will work out in our favor. Ever been in a group project with a chronic micromanager? We are literally those people in a group project...with Jesus, who's already taken this class before and passed. Matter of fact, He's teaching the course. Yet and still, we don't believe He has the credentials. It sounds crazy, I know, but this is what we do to our Father every day.

I realized later on in my dream-chasing journey that I didn't know how to be a content passenger. I didn't know how to leave room for God. I would fake give Him the wheel, but quickly take it back when the road got too bumpy or seemed to be taking an unauthorized detour.

Eventually, I got tired of myself and decided it was time to not only be a passenger but take it a step further by climbing into the back seat to take a much-needed nap. I've been riding in the backseat ever since. Every time I feel the need to correct the speed or offer a shortcut, I see Jesus' eyes look lovingly but sternly in the rearview mirror and without saying a word, I already know what I need to do.

It hasn't been easy. There have been plenty of roads where I looked out the window with displeasure at the route He was taking.

Surely there's a shortcut.
He definitely could have made a left on Michigan Ave.
Sheila went that way and look at her life! Oprah knows her name.

Soon enough, I find that there was a pit stop He needed me to make to give me the tools for the next leg of the journey, and it all makes sense.

Chill out.
Be Still, Darling.
Let God be God.

Recall a time you attempted to do something
without God. How did it turn out?
What did it feel like?

Application

In the past, what have you believed is impossible, even for God? (Be honest. He can take it.)

Application

Why are you rushing?

Who/what are you competing with?

DATE

Note to Self

Numbers 17:8 (KJV)

And it came to pass, that on the morrow Moses went into the tabernacle of witness; and, behold, the rod of Aaron for the house of Levi was budded, and brought forth buds, and bloomed blossoms, and yielded almonds.

Psalm 46:10

Be still, and know that I am God; I will be exalted among the nations,

I will be exalted in the earth.

Matthew 5:16 (KJV)

Let your light shine before others, so that they may see your good works and give glory to your Father who is in heaven

Ezekiel 28:13–15 NKJV

You were in Eden, the garden of God; Every precious stone was your covering: The sardius, topaz, and diamond, Beryl, onyx, and jasper, Sapphire, turquoise, and emerald with gold. The workmanship of your timbrels and pipes Was prepared for you on the day you were created. You were the anointed cherub who covers; I established you; You were on the holy mountain of God; You walked back and forth in the midst of fiery stones. You were perfect in your ways from the day you were created, Till iniquity was found in you.

Psalm 10:4 (NIV)

In his pride the wicked does not seek him;
in all his thoughts there is no room for God.

NOTE TO SELF

I will allow Him, who can "do exceedingly and abundantly above all that we ask or think," to move on my behalf. I will follow the steps He has outlined for me in the exact order. He knows better than I. I will not run ahead, nor will I count myself out before the race is over. I will cultivate patience and work on being a light for others rather than hoarding it all for myself. I will, above all things, lead others to Christ using the dream He gave me as a catalyst, all for His glory. I will blossom, bloom, and produce purpose based on His timeline and not my own.

Week 3

Be Satisfied in Jesus (and not just in His provision).

HE MUST INCREASE, BUT I MUST DECREASE.
JOHN 3:30 (KJV)

I KNOW WHAT IT IS TO BE IN NEED, AND I KNOW WHAT IT IS TO HAVE PLENTY. I HAVE LEARNED THE SECRET OF BEING CONTENT IN ANY AND EVERY SITUATION, WHETHER WELL FED OR HUNGRY, WHETHER LIVING IN PLENTY OR IN WANT. I CAN DO ALL THIS THROUGH HIM WHO GIVES ME STRENGTH
PHILLIPIANS 14:12-13 (NIV)

This week we are finally breaking down the term Anti-Hustle. I'm sure you've been curious by now. What does it mean? Where did it come from? Why is it so important?

For a long time, I had a hard time understanding my purpose. Although He had given me to outline, I was searching for meaning and ignored the most important one that was right under my nose: The call to motherhood and wifehood.

I neglected my first role in search of fulfillment elsewhere, searching for applause and accolades. Essentially, I fell into the "girl-boss" brainwash and believed a meme that said

"We all have the same 24 hours as Oprah and Beyonce-- do better."

I would often stay up until 3, 4, or 5 am for extended periods—and when I say extended, I mean several years trying to keep up with Lady O and Queen B. I believed it was the only road to success, and I blindly followed and had nothing left for my family or myself.

After fainting spells, overwhelming anxiety, depression, and frustration, I felt God calling me out of the darkness. He showed me that so many are "high-achieving" and driven but not necessarily doing so in alignment with His Word.

My business was known for making custom pillows, candles and gift boxes. I often received orders from a celebrity or social media influencers team to help send thank you gifts to their clients. Sometimes I had to deliver them by hand. I would get excited knowing I was on my way to meet someone that so many revered and would pay thousands to be in the same room with.

Once I started meeting some of my favorite celebs and social influencers in person, I started to notice the same pattern. They were happy on camera, but their real lives were plagued with sadness. It was such a jarring visual to see a grown woman with a million followers tell me she was miserable. I didn't understand. How could you be at the height of your career and not be ecstatic?

We are so proud to be known and identified as "a hustler," but few understand the full repercussions behind that lifestyle. If we did, we wouldn't want it. I used to date people who were real *hustlers*. As in it was their occupation and only source of income. Let me tell you, when the FBI is looking for you, hustling can go from admirable to unsafe very quickly. I know someone out there can identify.

On top of that, Beyoncé and Oprah have a FULL team at their beck and call 24 hours a day and seemingly UNLIMITED financial resources. No ma'am. Our 24 hours are NOT the same. Whoever created that quote and turned it into a shareable image straight lied and deceived us all. I'm mad I thought it was cute and didn't think it all the way through.

The deception of trying to be Beyonce began to take over areas that were supposed to be non-negotiable. I'm ashamed to say, I disappeared in the middle of my child's 3rd birthday party to fulfill a pending order. I snuck out of church in the middle of service several times to run to the post office. I turned down date nights with my husband and outings with my closest friends to fix something on my website or meet with one of my suppliers.

I religiously listened to my favorite podcast, NPR's *How I Built This*, dreaming of the day I would be the one to be the interviewed on the show. Instead of focusing on my spiritual growth, marriage, and raising my babies, I focused on building an empire by any means necessary. I wanted to be Sarah Blakey of Spanx or Myleik Teele of Curlbox and it was my main goal. I convinced myself that my family could wait because someday they would thank me for all the sacrifices, I had made...for them.

The idea of having a purpose became intertwined with being useful. Usefulness, to me, meant I had to be hyper-focused on productivity. It was a sink or swim mentality. There was no time to float.

I wish I would have known that the hustle is a treadmill that leads to nowhere. Even if it looks like others have made it, I'm not sure I would have been able to make the same, often ruthless, decisions they had to make. Something always gives. It has to. The sacrifice isn't always worth the reward.

Let's define the Anti-Hustle by breaking it into parts. First, the meaning of the word HUSTLE compiled from several dictionaries*:

Hustle [huhs-uhl]

-a dishonest plan for getting money (SCAM)

-to obtain money by fraud or deception (MANIPULATION)

-to sell something to or obtain something from (someone) by energetic and especially underhanded activity (SWINDLE)

-to crowd or push roughly to convey forcibly or hurriedly (IMPATIENCE)

-to act quickly and with energy (i.e., the hustle and bustle of the city)

Therefore, the word ANTI-HUSTLE
is the converse to all of the above.

Anti-Hustle [an-tee - huhs-uh l]

a resistance to scamming, swindling, pushing, forcing, rushing, and attempting to manipulate God.

In addition to asking WHAT is Hustling, it may be beneficial to talk about four reasons we choose to Hustle. We will cover two reasons this week and the additional ones next week.

#1

We lack an accurate view of eternity and would much rather spend the rest of our lives wealthy on earth then in pursuit of heaven.

<u>HUSTLE</u>: INCREASE

<u>THE ANTI HUSTLE:</u> DECREASE

Our entire goal on earth is to be comfortable. We want nothing more than to be rich and famous. Even when we pretend that we want to be wealthy to "help other people," somewhere deep down on the inside, there is another more worldly ulterior motivation. Tell the truth. Philanthropy is on the list but only after you buy your 15-bedroom house.

We want to be rich to bless other people **AND** show our mama, and everyone who else who hated on us that we made it. It is very rarely a pure and honest thought process.

In the meantime, we flock to pastors who pray against the generational curse of poverty and offer prophetic words of abundance. In contrast, when was the last time you heard those pastors prayers against sexual immorality, promiscuity, secrecy, manipulation, anger, greed or unforgiveness? I'm sure it happens, but it's infrequent.

Often, doing the heart work (see Week 1) and asking God for a clean heart is too burdensome. Instead, it's easier to seek prayer over our bank account rather than prayers for our lack of empathy for the poor, the fact that you don't know how to be single, or the hatred you still have in your heart for an absentee mother.

The truth is, we want to believe when God is referencing the word "blessing" that He is referring ONLY to money. That's the only kind of blessing we think is worthwhile. We want to be rich and elevated at all costs, even if it costs us our lives and a relationship with our Father.

A definition of *blessing* is the enjoyment of God's divine favor. Favor can be riches, but it can also be emotional-mental-spiritual health, and so much more. Don't get me wrong. I believe in a God who owns all the cattle on a thousand hills, a God who can make money appear out of nowhere and make it rain dollar bills, a God who can use the wealthy to bless the poor and change the world.

However, as Ecclesiastes 3 tells us, *"there is a time for everything."* There are seasons of increase and seasons of decrease. Guess which one most of us would prefer? I'm here to tell you that there are just as many blessings in the "decrease" season as there are in the "increase" season.

He must increase, but I must decrease.
John 3:30 (KJV)

When was the last time you prayed a "decrease me" prayer? How about a "hide me until YOU see fit" request? I know. It doesn't even sound right. It comes off as if you lack faith to believe for more. At least that's what the internet preachers tell us. If you're like me, you prefer the Prayer of Jabez that specifically asks for an increase:

> Oh, that you would bless me and enlarge my border, and that your hand might be with me, and that you would keep me from harm so that it might not bring me pain!
> 1 Chronicles 4:10 (ESV)

This is the life we prefer to live—one filled with blessings, no harm, and no pain. He **can** do it, but what do we do with times God says, "No" or "Wait" or "You're going to have to go through a valley first?" Nobody fully equips us for that response. How does one deal with a straight up **NO** from an emotional standpoint?

A friend once suggested a book *(thank you Leah)* that has changed my entire outlook on the way God is leading and molding us to be able to fully receive and enjoy what He has in store. It's called *Hinds Feet on High Places* by Hanna Hurnard.

It starts off reading like a child's fairy tale and so, I won't even lie, I would put it down often just not getting the point. I ended up reading it one evening out of pure boredom and for some reason, I saw something I had never seen before. The main character, Much-Afraid, was me.

I mean, I was her.

I mean, she was all of us trying to make it. Whenever something went wrong, she would cry out for help. Sometimes the help didn't come the way she expected it to. Sometimes it wasn't an immediate escape. There was a hardship she had to go through, and it was painful. (If you're wondering, Yes, I'm asking you to find the book and read it for yourself. It's life changing.)

There's a verse I want to share that strangely gives me comfort:

In the days of his flesh, Jesus offered up prayers and supplications, with loud cries and tears, to him who was able to save him from death, and he was heard because of his reverence.
Hebrews 5:7 (ESV)

It's crazy to think about, but even Jesus was denied his prayer request. He went before the Father and begged and well, we all know what happened next. The reason He was declined was because there was something bigger that had to be done. Something with long-term and far reaching consequences. What if our NO is just to be able to fulfill something that has long reaching consequences for someone else?

truth bomb

A "decrease" isn't a punishment.

When we pray for increase (promotions, bigger homes, profit in our business, more children, health, a husband, notoriety, release from less than ideal situation) and it isn't coming as quickly as we assume it should, or even at all, we have to have enough faith to see God as the ultimate orchestrator. There *is* a reason. There is *always* a reason.

In these moments, we must have a view of eternity that reminds us that He is still God and still good. I know. It's hard, especially when everybody around you is increasing while you are barely making it, but Jesus understands. He gets it.

One evening I was crying out to God for deliverance from a season in which I was feeling lost and forgotten. I was doing all the things a good Christian is supposed to do and still felt like I was stuck on the losing team. He gently reminded me that I lived in a fallen world, which automatically dictated that there would be pain and suffering while here on earth. It is inevitable. Then, in the midst of my whining and moping, He leads me to a promise:

And the God of all grace, who called you to his eternal
glory in Christ, after you have suffered a little while, will
himself restore you and make you strong,
firm and steadfast.
1 Peter 5:10 (NIV)

With a full and clear view of eternity, we see every setback
or frustration as another way that God is forming our
character for our real Home that He is preparing for us.
We begin to see the "decrease" as necessary and
temporary and we know He's up to something major! Let
us learn to be satisfied in Him - and not just with His
provision.

#2

**We have to be seen by others to approve
and cosign the blessing.**

HUSTLE: INSTANT VISIBILITY

ANTI-HUSTLE: HIDDEN CONTENTMENT

I'm always super-interested in people who start dating someone for two weeks and then post about it on their social media. I need somebody to do a case study. I would love to read about the psychology behind it.

It always begins with subtleties hinting that there is someone else in the picture, like an extra shadow on the sidewalk or an additional table setting slightly out of frame. Then, a few posts later we get to see his handsome face and her huge smile. *She looks so happy! We're excited!* By now, we are fully invested in the happiness of our insta-friend (whom we may have never actually met in real life). We "like" all her posts and comment on how the gift she got him for Christmas was *perfect*!

Then, suddenly, 2 months in, with no warning, all his pictures disappear. Now we're sad because we were looking forward to watching the wedding on Instagram Live!

What makes us *rush* to show the world before we have discerned if this is a show and tell season or a hidden season?

I believe it is because we no longer believe in the process of planting/sowing, watering, waiting, and then reaping privately. We have lost the art of abiding in Him, allowing something to be fully grown and fertilized by Christ before being revealed to the world.

The Bible gives us the best example of staying hidden until the time is right. Luke records the birth of Jesus, the 8th day, 12 years old, and then straight to his baptism by John the Baptist.

Wait.
Hold up.

Question: What was Jesus doing from the 8th day to age 12 and from age 12 to 31?

Answer: It doesn't matter. It wasn't "the appointed time."

In other words, He was chillin'—waiting for His heavenly cue, "Annnnd Action!!"

As soon as He knew He was the lead actor in the next scene, my Dude said, *I'm ready* and showed up right on time to be baptized. How? Because He had been practicing and memorizing His lines in obscurity, away from the limelight

truth bomb

Elevation simply means to be visible and to come out hiding; it doesn't always come with a microphone, a stage and a spotlight. It could mean a seat at the table, but you may not be the host.

What dream have you harvested before it had time to take root fully? You plucked it to put in the window for all to see, and God was like, *"Baby girl! What are you doing? It's not time yet! If you had just waited a little while longer, I could have created something beautiful."*

How many opportunities have we missed because we rushed ahead of Him before the cake was fully baked? How grieved He must be by our hurry to impress our friends over obedience.

I've been a stay-at-home mom longer than I've ever had a working career.

When I was at home, I wished I was at work.

When at work, I wished I was at home investing in my business.

When I was working on my business, I wished I was spending more time with my kids.

When I was spending more time with my kids, I wished I had spent that time with my husband.

When I spent time with my husband, I wished I could spend some time by myself.

I was never satisfied with where God had me during that season—always looking for the next, always searching for something that could fulfill me more than what was in front of me. In hindsight, I should have spent more time noticing the small blessings in front of me. My character could have used a healthy dose of contentment. Contentment pushes away the need to rush. It makes hustling feel futile and unnecessary.

I need us (and please know I have to check myself daily on this) to re-examine what we are asking for when we seek visibility, favor, elevation, wealth, abundance, etc. Why do we need it to be of use to God? The idea that the janitor or the secretary is somehow worth less than the CEO is crazy. You certainly notice their absence when they are gone, right?

It is in the perceived boring and mundane tasks that we are tested. It is in the responsibilities that seem pointless, but are crucial to our spiritual development, that we see who rises to the top. Call it whatever you please, but at its core, it is simply patience and humility.

Everything doesn't have to be applauded to be significant. Just because nobody saw it, it doesn't mean it wasn't relevant. Your purpose isn't fueled by applause, and in some cases, applause is what kills it. Instead, it is discovered and built in small, every day, and often unseen character-building actions. The Anti-Hustle means staying hidden (and content) until God elevates you, **if** thats what He deems best.

The "*If*" in the previous sentence brings me to my last point. There are so many of us that are not given a platform because it would ultimately lead us astray. We would end up making decisions along the way that would be in clear opposition to our faith—creeping and slow leak compromises that wouldn't seem so bad in the beginning but are still out of alignment with Gods word.

But godliness with contentment is great gain. For we brought nothing into the world, and we can take nothing out of it. But if we have food and clothing, we will be content with that. People who want to get rich fall into temptation and a trap and into many foolish and harmful desires that plunge men into ruin and destruction. For the love of money is a root of all kinds of evil. Some people, eager for money, have wandered from the faith and pierced themselves with many griefs. But you, man of God, flee from all this, and pursue righteousness, godliness, faith, love, endurance and gentleness. 1 Timothy 6:6-11 (NIV)

To ensure we make it to heaven, which is the goal, we may never be "seen" outside of reaching the small community of people entrusted to us. In this regard, elevation isn't the wealth we all prefer, rather it is being known in our home, our neighborhoods, our jobs, or serving in the parking lot of the local church. It is living a full and content life that isn't seen or cosigned by others outside of God. It is being rich in heart and spirit.

All of it is important. Every moment means something.
Nothing goes unnoticed by God.
Nothing is mundane or trivial.

Your contentment and abiding in Christ is worth its weight in gold. Whew! If that didn't shift your mindset, I don't know what will!

Application

What would a "decrease me" prayer look like for you?

Application

How could you better spend the hours you would typically spend "striving" and "pushing" and trying to force something to happen?

What are some mundane and boring tasks that you have written off as useless but are actually helpful for character development?

Note to Self

John 3:30 (KJV)

He must increase, but I must decrease.

Philippians 14:12-13 (NIV)

I know what it is to be in need, and I know what it is to have plenty. I have learned the secret of being content in any and every situation, whether well fed or hungry, whether living in plenty or in want. I can do all this through him who gives me strength

1 Chronicles 4:10 (ESV)

Oh, that you would bless me and enlarge my border, and that your hand might be with me, and that you would keep me from harm so that it might not bring me pain!

Hebrews 5:7 (ESV)

In the days of his flesh, Jesus offered up prayers and supplications, with loud cries and tears, to him who was able to save him from death, and he was heard because of his reverence.

1 Peter 5:10 (NIV)

And the God of all grace, who called you to his eternal glory in Christ, after you have suffered a little while, will himself restore you and make you strong, firm and steadfast.

1 Timothy 6:6-11 (NIV)

But godliness with contentment is great gain.
For we brought nothing into the world, and we can take nothing out of it. But if we have food and clothing, we will be content with that. People who want to get rich fall into temptation and a trap and into many foolish and harmful desires that plunge men into ruin and destruction. For the love of money is a root of all kinds of evil. Some people, eager for money, have wandered from the faith and pierced themselves with many griefs. But you, man of God, flee from all this, and pursue righteousness, godliness, faith, love, endurance and gentleness.

Week #3

NOTE TO SELF

I will learn to like myself, so that views and comments don't become my marker for success. I am satisfied knowing that God has something greater for me. That "greater" may still be underground, but I'm willing to wait. While waiting, I will practice being present in friendships, marriage, family, self-care, and other areas of my life that are easily neglected while chasing my goals. When all is said and done, His praise will continually be on my lips because He is a good Father. I am blessed and highly favored, no matter the season.

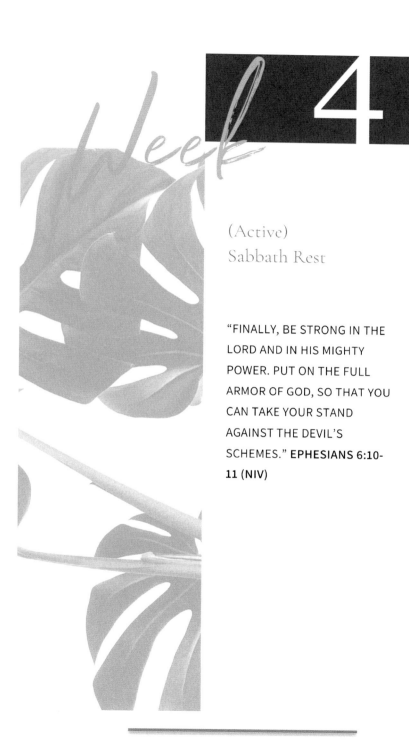

Week

4

(Active)
Sabbath Rest

"FINALLY, BE STRONG IN THE
LORD AND IN HIS MIGHTY
POWER. PUT ON THE FULL
ARMOR OF GOD, SO THAT YOU
CAN TAKE YOUR STAND
AGAINST THE DEVIL'S
SCHEMES." **EPHESIANS 6:10-
11 (NIV)**

Last week we discussed two reasons hustling has become such a cultural norm. This week we are covering two more that are essential in our pursuit of the anti-hustle lifestyle.

#3

We take the 4th commandment as a suggestion rather than a commandment.

HUSTLE: Rest-less/Anxious

ANTI-HUSTLE: Rest

Remember the Sabbath day, to keep it holy. Six days shalt thou labor, and do all thy work: But the seventh day is the Sabbath of the Lord thy God: in it thou shalt not do any work, thou, nor thy son, nor thy daughter, thy manservant, nor thy maidservant, nor thy cattle, nor thy stranger that is within thy gates: For in six days the Lord made heaven and earth, the sea, and all that in them is, and rested the seventh day: wherefore the Lord blessed the Sabbath day, and hallowed it.
Exodus 20:8 (KJV)

Yes. That is the exact wording of a direct command from God. Commandment number 4 of a list that is fundamental to the Christian faith. Why do we spend so much time focusing on thou shall not lie, thou shall not commit adultery etc. and completely ignore the 4th commandment like it's nonexistent? Yes, the others are important, but doesn't it seem like its dismissed more than mandated?

I know some people pick a day to take Sabbath rest, but did you know there is an ACTUAL Sabbath day? Long story short, it has always been Saturday, and then it was changed to Sunday somewhere in history and stuck as a tradition over time.

Google it. You'll see. The Sabbath wasn't just relegated to people in the Jewish faith. It has been celebrated by Christ followers for generations until a group of religious lawmakers decided it was an inconvenience.

Some people may refer to it as an "Old Covenant Law," but I would implore you to fully do your research. You will see that the Sabbath became optional for us over time (due to man made interpretation and traditions) but it never ceased to be of utmost importance to God. Whatever is important to Him should be important to us too, right?

My family and I choose to worship on the Biblical Sabbath. We aren't alone. Several hundreds of thousands of families choose to do the same. But to be honest, even those of us that rest on the Biblical Sabbath from Friday at sunset to Saturday at sunset aren't resting WELL.

Rest doesn't come naturally to our flesh, but He gave us an order. Work 6 days. Rest 1 day. (Think about it as a tithe). There is a reason He was adamant about putting rest in The Commandments. God started by saying, *REMEMBER* because He knew we would forget! Every other commandment starts off with "Thou Shall not…". There's this ONE verse that not only has a different opening, it also comes with specifics. Why would God, through Moses, take the time to explain in detail. There's got to be something to that.

Sabbath rest is not an option, and it isn't negotiable. He requires it. He wants it for us because He knows what it can do for us physically, emotionally, mentally, and spiritually.

A lot of us are sick because we don't know how to turn off. How toxic is that? We were not created to keep moving indefinitely. Even those on "Team No Sleep" can't maintain that level of productivity long term. Advocates for the hustle are forced to lay down eventually.

God who knew enough about me in the future to include a unique mandate—

STOP.
REALIGN.
REMEMBER ME.
REST.

It's amazing. He accounted for the hustle and bustle of life and knew we, much like the second generation of Israelites in the desert, would need a weekly reminder that He is in control.

Don't dismiss that. Your flesh may want to put it away on the back burner because,

How is it possible to give God one entire day? or
Traditionally I go to church then do whatever I want for the rest of the day.
He's okay with that, isn't He?

I know what the answer is, but I think there are some inquiries that need to be taken to God in prayer yourself. There are some questions that need to go straight to the source so that you can get a direct response. I am wondering though, if the answer you get back will be something you embrace. Are you willing to change your lifestyle in obedience?

It feels l old an archaic and like He's asking for a lot, but is He? It's a personal relationship thing, so I won't belabor the point, but the fact that you were drawn to this book tells me that your soul is thirsty for something more.
I encourage you to try it. I would love to find out how it felt to tithe on the time He's given you. You are being called to rest when everyone else is running. It's a real-life turtle and hare race situation, and we all know how that turned out. Do you trust God enough to give Him 24 hours out of your 168 hour week?

#4

We assume stillness is an excuse for lack of Proactivity or Productivity...

HUSTLE: RUNNING (IN CIRCLES)

ANTI-HUSTLE: (ACTIVE) STILLNESS

... instead, it is a heightened awareness of who GOD is. For the record, Satan does not care about your health, wealth, family, or relationships. He doesn't care that you are tired or overworked. All he wants for you and from you is your unbelief or doubt in Jesus Christ.

Ironically, the more tired you are, the more overwhelmed you become, and the less time you have to be still in Christ. Ultimately leading to doubt, fear, and lack of faith. Hustling is his way of lowering your shield of faith just enough for him to get to your heart. Ephesians 6 says it this way:

> Finally, be strong in the Lord and in his mighty power. Put on the full armor of God, so that you can take your stand against the devil's schemes.
> 6:10-11 (NIV)

The enemy attacks by attempting to scheme us into putting down a vital piece of our armory:

In addition to all this, take up the shield of faith,
with which you can extinguish all the
flaming arrows of the evil one
(verse 16)

The idea of using faith to fuel productivity is not a popular one but keeping the shield of faith in position at all times keeps us in alignment. Without it, we are prone to misunderstanding simple concepts that are ultimately life-giving (like Sabbath rest).

The adversary is keeping us busy chasing our own tails. The more aimlessly active we are, the more that imp and his minions can convince us that we don't need Jesus.

I believe we have a hard time being still because it reminds us of a perpetual "Easy Like Sunday Morning" vibe swinging on the front porch. The perfect breeze. A glass of freshly squeezed lemonade. No plans. No direction. No drive. No vision. No strategy.

For people that are used to being busy, it screams lazy. It smells like indecisiveness. It looks like fear of getting in the ring for the big fight.

I am proposing to you that Biblical stillness *IS* busy, hard-work, and deliberate. I like to call it Active Stillness.

Here, at this moment, is typically the place where people push back. They have a hard time understanding how stillness doesn't mean stagnation.

Every Instagram influencer, strategist, motivational speaker, teacher, preacher (you name it), is yelling, *DO MORE! BE MORE! DON'T STOP!*

Underneath all that babble is an exhausted man or woman who doesn't even buy into their *own* sales pitch. Don't believe the hype.

It's not realistic.

What I mean by stillness is more than just sitting idly by doing nothing; it is waiting on the cue from God as He directs the next strategic move. It is raising your shield in anticipation.

While waiting, you are preparing, studying, discerning, watching, asking, praying, and worshipping. These are all extremely active words. While waiting, you are watching to make sure you don't miss what God is doing. That sounds far from laziness to me! I believe they call it working smarter and not harder.

I wish I would have learned this concept early in my entrepreneurial journey. I made a big mistake because I missed what God was doing. It took me longer than it should have to finally see it was all my fault.

After being at home mom with my babies for several years, I decided it was time to get back into the workforce. I prayed for a job and after a full year of interviews, I finally got a job! I was excited! Real life adult conversations by the water-cooler! I couldn't wait.

It wasn't the best salary by any means, but I was excited to finally get out of the house. I was overly qualified for the job and so most tasks were completed faster than what was expected of me. I found shortcuts and created systems for everything which got me noticed. I received two promotions in the first six months, AND they wanted to continue to promote me overlooking the required certifications! (Talk about favor!). Then just like that, with no warning, I quit.

After feeling overly confident that I had heard from God and I was supposed to start a business, I wrote my two-weeks resignation and left. In my defense, it was 2015 and the trigger word was "side-hustle." If you didn't have one that could replace your full-time income, then something was wrong. I knew a few entrepreneurs who had made it big after quitting and so I decided that was the avenue Jesus wanted me to take too.

Well, instead of waiting for full instructions, I started running at my own pace. Okay, so I say running like it was a light jog. It was a full sprint. I was OFF. I didn't even look back to confirm. Talk about bad timing and underestimating the formation of character.

- I quit in the middle of a school year leaving teachers and other administrators scrambling to find a replacement.

- I quit without ensuring that I had enough in our bank account to cover our family for at least six months. We went down to one income within two weeks with two children under the age three.

- I quit without thoroughly researching the process of making and shipping handmade products. No business plans. No market research. No plan B.

- I did not wait for clarity or confirmation, I simply assumed it's what He wanted for me.

It took me four years to figure out what I'm now convinced He could have taught me in under a week. I look back on it now, and I'm like, *Sethlina. Honey. Baby Girl. What were you thinking?*

I believe God was trying to set up provision so that I could work and pour into a side gig over time, but I was determined to do it my way.

Again, in my defense, I truly believed that I had heard God say, *Do it now.* In hindsight, it may have been, *Start preparing now, I will show you the way out later.* I took matters into my own hands and figured he would see how hard I was working in His name. Unknowingly, I was running in circles when all He wanted was for me to focus on the doors He had already opened while waiting for the go ahead in other areas.

Active stillness is a real thing. Trusting God with His plans for your life is hard work yet wholly fulfilling, and if that's what "lazy" looks like, I'm here for it with a full cup of a lemonade and a perfect breeze.

Application

How can you put Sabbath rest in your weekly schedule?

Where do you find yourself racing in a full
sprint instead of a leisurely walk?
Who/what are you racing against?

DATE

Note to Self

Ephesians 6:10-11 (NIV)

Finally, be strong in the Lord and in his mighty power. Put on the full armor of God, so that you can take your stand against the devil's schemes

Exodus 20:8 (KJV)

Remember the Sabbath day, to keep it holy. Six days shalt thou labour, and do all thy work: But the seventh day is the Sabbath of the Lord thy God: in it thou shalt not do any work, thou, nor thy son, nor thy daughter, thy manservant, nor thy maidservant, nor thy cattle, nor thy stranger that is within thy gates: For in six days the Lord made heaven and earth, the sea, and all that in them is, and rested the seventh day: wherefore the Lord blessed the Sabbath day, and hallowed it.

Ephesians 6:16 (NIV)

In addition to all this, take up the shield of faith, with which you can extinguish all the flaming arrows of the evil one

Week #4

NOTE TO SELF

I reject the notion that resting and stillness
is somehow less effective then hustling. The
truth is, waiting for God's instructions is
another way of stewarding my gifts, talents
and dreams and there is no shame in that.
As a matter of fact, it is noble and Biblical. In
the meantime, I am putting on the whole
armor of God while watching, praying and
worshipping, seeking discernment on His
will for my life and finding joy in true
Sabbath Rest.

Conclusion

God pictures himself as a mountain spring of clean, cool, life-giving water. The way to glorify a fountain like this is to enjoy the water, and praise the water, and keep coming back to the water, and point other people to the water, and get strength for love from the water, and never, never, never prefer any drink in the world over this water. -John Piper, *When I Don't Desire God*

Over the past ten years, I have dreamed big dreams that God didn't cosign and made it an idol. The idea that it could satisfy me outside of the Dream Giver is bogus. How dare I put anything before the all-powerful God- and yet I did. Over and over again. I was thirsty for ambition, aspirations, goals, dreams, visions, hopes desires without stopping to ask God if this was what He had in mind for me.

Part of the blueprint Jesus gave me that night revealed that I would be in the marketplace of some sort. I could see myself creating and selling products in conjunction with a ministry. As you already know, I went about it the wrong way and suffered the consequences, but it all happened! It all came to fruition. I took the long way to get there, *but* it happened! I created an online store selling pillows, blankets, candles, and other home lifestyle products as a Christian entrepreneur.

He had done it, just like He said.

That is until I started drinking something outside of the cool water He was already supplying. I convinced myself that I was doing so well that God wanted me to have a storefront. I decided I was supposed to have a boutique, and I started major business decisions from that point of view. I began to scale quicker than I should have and started adding products to my online store in preparation for a future brick and mortar. Did He tell me I would have a brick and mortar flagship store? Not exactly, but undoubtedly it was the next step. I thought to myself, *He is a good Father and wants to enlarge my territory*

I am not even exaggerating. The minute I started detouring off course and making plans that weren't entirely legitimate, I started losing control of all of it. The business, the ministry, my family life, friendships, health---all of it began to implode on itself. Talk about crashing and burning.

I came across a quote while reading a book and I knew that God was talking to me:

If you start something and it does not seem to go well, consider carefully that God, on purpose, may not be authenticating what you told the people because it did not come from Him, but from your own head.

You may have wanted to do something outstanding for God and forgot that God does not want that. He wants you to be available to Him, and more importantly, to be obedient to Him. - Henry Blackaby, *Experiencing God*

Years of me trying to do "something outstanding for God" had turned this dream into something I didn't even recognize. I was flabbergasted. I was doing it all for Him! Why didn't He bless it?

In writing this mini-devotional, I became worried that it would come off as a self-help manual. You know, those books that teach you how to make a million dollars or how to fall in love. I don't have the fool-proof instructions on any of this dream stuff. I cannot implicitly say that you will get on this anti-hustle journey and God will magically make all your dreams come true. Instead, in true God fashion, He is using this journey to draw us unto Himself.

In your rush to implement these principles into your life, I am begging that you caution against running ahead before authenticating your new-found clarity with your Maker. Please make sure it's not in your head. Please make sure you aren't bringing Him more than He requested of you.

Let me try explaining it another way.

My 5-year-old daughter has a way of bringing me things that I didn't ask for to find a way to be in my presence (or be nosey and listen to my conversation with her father).

Suddenly, she is convinced that I am thirsty and mysteriously appears with a glass of water I didn't send for her to bring me. She shows up with my phone that I purposely left charging in another room. She gets my purse, *"Just in case you need to buy something, mommy."* Meanwhile, I'm in my pajamas, watching Netflix. There is no sign of me going to the store and no laptop or phone to indicate I'm shopping online. If I respond that I didn't ask her to bring me anything, she acts hurt and retorts, *"I was just trying to help!"*

This is how God sees us. We are convinced that God must need us to <insert your dream/aspiration here>, and we dive right in expecting Him to bless it. That's not what He asked for.

As you know by now, He is way more concerned with your character, stewardship over the little He has given, obedience, integrity etc. If we fail at being first a foremost a Christ-follower seeking holiness, we have failed it all. What else is there to bring him but open hands asking to be used by Him in whatever capacity that may be.

If you take nothing else from these pages, I need you to know that God's enoughness is just that. Enough. Not only because we did the heart work.

Not just because we finally allowed Him to do what he does best. Not just because we find contentment and implement Biblical Sabbath rest.

God is enough because He is all we will ever need, with or without our dreams. I don't know where the Anti-Hustle is going to take you. I don't know if you are applying this to your home life, business, marriage, friendships, or anything else that calls us to dream bigger. What I do know is that God is in it. Whatever it is. He's right there in the highs and certainly in the lows. He's there in seasons where you must bust your butt to get it done, and in seasons where laying in bed is the only thing on the list.

I pray that on your journey, you continue to seek Him, and only Him, in the midst of it all.

Don't love the world's ways. Don't love the world's goods. Love of the world squeezes out love for the Father. Practically everything that goes on in the world — wanting your own way, wanting everything for yourself, wanting to appear important — has nothing to do with the Father. It just isolates you from him. The world and all its wanting, wanting, wanting is on the way out — but whoever does what God wants is set for eternity.

1 John 2:16-17 (MSG)

Reflections

Antihustle
MANIFESTO

I will not use the vision He gave me as a test of His goodness or faithfulness. He is GOD with or without my dream. He delights in giving me my heart's desire, but I will not forget whose desires they are to begin with. I will allow my character to be pruned and heart to be purified in preparation for what is to come. I will REST in the promise, knowing that it will come to pass, and He doesn't need my help to do so.

I will allow Him, who can "do exceedingly and abundantly above all that we ask or think," to move on my behalf. I will follow the steps He has outlined for me in the exact order. He knows better than I. I will not run ahead, nor will I count myself out before the race is over. I will cultivate patience and work on being a light for others rather than hoarding it all for myself. I will, above all things, lead others to Christ using the dream He gave me as a catalyst, all for His glory. I will blossom, bloom, and produce purpose based on His timeline and not my own.

I will learn to like myself, so that views and comments don't become my marker for success. I am satisfied knowing that God has something greater for me. That "greater" may still be underground, but I'm willing to wait. While waiting, I will practice being present in friendships, marriage, family, self-care, and other areas of my life that are easily neglected while chasing my goals. When all is said and done, His praise will continually be on my lips because He is a good Father. I am blessed and highly favored, no matter the season.

I reject the notion that resting and stillness is somehow less effective then hustling. The truth is, waiting for God's instructions is another way of stewarding my gifts, talents and dreams and there is no shame in that. As a matter of fact, it is noble and Biblical. In the meantime, I am putting on the whole armor of God while watching, praying and worshipping, seeking discernment on His will for my life and finding joy in true Sabbath Rest.

"God is within her, she will not fall; God will help her at break of day.

Sethlina Amakye
Author, Speaker, and Designer

Sethlina is a Kingdom-focused multi-passionate maker, designer, word nerd and all-around creative. She is obsessed with what it means to live "well" and on purpose. More specifically, she create devotionals, gifts, home decor products, and designs interior spaces that serve as a daily (and pretty) reminder of whose we are.

Made in the USA
Monee, IL
09 June 2020